grit

kindling

to relight the wounded and weary

SHANNON GUERRA

A bruised reed he will not break,
and a faintly burning wick
he will not quench;
he will faithfully bring forth justice.
– Isaiah 42:3

ISBN 979-8-9887158-4-9
eISBN 979-8-9887158-5-6

Published by Copperlight Wood
P.O. Box 298086
Wasilla, AK
99629
www.copperlightwood.com

Cover photo by Gleb Lukomets via Unsplash

Design and all other photography by Shannon Guerra

Unless noted otherwise, scripture quotations are from the ESV® Bible (The Holy Bible, English Standard Version®), copyright © 2001 by Crossway, a publishing ministry of Good News Publishers. Used by permission. All rights reserved.

Portions of scripture in **bold** are the author's emphasis.

contents

yes, it will be messy

If you could see the mess on my desk, you wouldn't want to. Stacks of papers and books, a few packets of garden seeds, scattered pens, and usually at least one empty coffee cup, water glass, or lunch dish, plus a toy that a kid deposited. And also a cat who thinks I work for her.

Here's what I need to remember, and maybe you do too: Taking on anything important is likely to be messier and more complicated than you imagine it will be. And that's okay.

It doesn't necessarily mean you're doing it wrong. It means you're learning. It means you're not in control, and you're going to have to trust the One who is.

"But if it's messy, people will see my imperfections," we think. So we refuse to move forward at all. Our pride keeps us from obedience, and our insecurity costs us (and others) the joy that would have come from that obedience.

Yes, it will probably be messy. You'll have to clean the desk, walk in grace, try again, forgive others, and forge on.

But that's how we get where we're going.

When we go hiking, we can't get to the summit if we're constantly looking at our shoes and wiping the dirt off them. We must look forward and keep moving our feet.

In Alaska, before spring comes, we experience breakup when the snow melts. It looks terrible and gross. Everything thaws fast in 45-degree days and it takes a while to dry out. The mud is squelchy, dirt everywhere, nothing is green yet, and it takes at least a month before things start to move that direction.

We have to endure this season to get to the flowers and harvest ahead, though. It's coming. We can't dig in the garden yet but there are other things we can do, like clean debris, start seeds inside, learn new things, and adjust our ways.

The ugly, bare season doesn't last forever. Beautiful green growth is coming. So much is happening underneath that we can't see, and God is doing miracles in us in the meantime as we look toward Him.

Then when the leaves are starting to bud, that magical spring growth lasts about a week: pale green leaves, filigree in the cottonwoods. But it doesn't look that way for long; the color of new growth doesn't accurately reflect what the end result will be. Those new buds leave catkins and husks everywhere in their sudden movement and expansion, because acceleration is messy, too.

Acceleration and growth don't look like what the final product will look like.

Does God expect us to figure these things out perfectly, immediately, with flawless sterility? No. Then why do we expect that of ourselves?

So if you are feeling like the Lord is moving you into high gear, give yourself (and everyone else) plenty of grace. The sap is running. Your leaves are growing. This is a messy, magical period that might be over quicker than you expect, and you'll be left with memories of the rush while finally seeing how far your branches can reach, and what they're meant to look like when the leaves are finally unfurled.

Where there are no oxen,
the manger is clean,
but abundant crops come
by the strength of the ox.
– Proverbs 14:4

Another thing that comes with spring in our neck of the woods is music recitals. One night, two of our kids were slated for performance: One played Batman, the other played Bach. One was super serious, the other was all smiles.

They both forgot to bow when they were finished. We cheered and clapped anyway.

Did it matter when one of them stumbled in the middle, had to get her bearings, and start going again? Did we clap less, or dock points? Of course not. We waited, praying, rooting for her, and sighed with relief when she kept going. That's our girl.

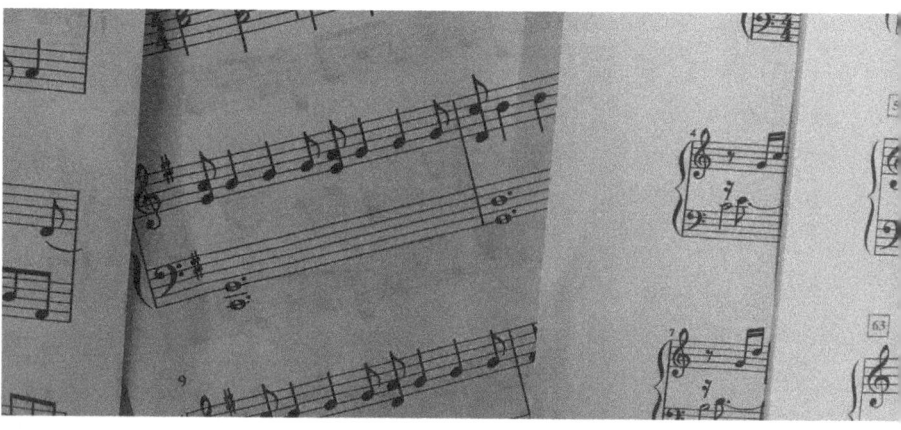

Did we scoff or complain when one of them forgot when to end, and repeated the last four measures two extra times? Did we look at our watches and wish he would finish already?

No way. We grinned and waited and grinned some more, knowing that he would get to that final dissonant chord soon enough, and he would look up with his lopsided dimples and triumph in his first public performance while we cheered.

Friend, if you are stumbling as you are trying something new and hard, your Father is not crossing His arms and looking at you in disappointment and disapproval.

He's not embarrassed by you. He's not bored or annoyed by you. He's so excited to watch you try and grow.

You are surrounded by a great cloud of witnesses cheering you on, pulling for you, making strides as you hit notes for the Kingdom. Even if it's only Batman today, they love the music because they know Bach is coming.

Your willingness to try and obey ignites cheers from heaven because it changes these days here on earth.

Therefore, since we are surrounded by so great a cloud of witnesses, let us also lay aside every weight, and sin which clings so closely, and let us run with endurance the race that is set before us, looking to Jesus, the founder and perfecter of our faith, who for the joy that was set before him endured the cross, despising the shame, and is seated at the right hand of the throne of God.

– Hebrews 12:1-2

Nor do people light a lamp and put it under a basket, but on a stand, and it gives light to all in the house. In the same way, let your light shine before others, so that they may see your good works and give glory to your Father who is in heaven.

– Matthew 5:16-17

A few nights after that recital, I listened to our daughter tackle a new song: the stops, the starts, the running through notes and then a quick stumble before picking up and going again.

But it was Beethoven, not Chopsticks.

She's growing and learning and pursuing. She masters a song and moves on to another. She's always working on several at once; some she's performed at recitals and some she's been practicing for almost a year, and others she picks up to try for the first time.

Mastery is not instant. It takes tons of hours, frustration, and persistence. It takes humility to let us hear her mistakes.

Really, will she ever think it's perfect? Do we ever feel like we've really arrived at mastering anything?

Nope. But she's learning.

And we are too, when we choose to grow.

> Do not neglect the gift you have, which was given you by prophecy when the council of elders laid their hands on you. Practice these things, immerse yourself in them, so that all may see your progress.
>
> – 1 Timothy 4:14-15

A word for the one who is tired & heartsick & wondering if things will get better:

Don't stop praying for that thing you're tempted to give up on. The Lord doesn't put good desires in your heart to tease you, but to show you where you're going.

Intercede for someone else while you wait, and use this time to bring life elsewhere, too.

Whoever brings blessing will be enriched,
and one who waters will himself be watered.
— Proverbs 11:25

He's not impatient or annoyed by you constantly asking Him if you're doing it right. He's not shaking His head and tsk-ing, wishing you'd get your act together and stop bugging Him. He's a good, good Father.

He loves your heart that continues to press forward in obedience and surrender, especially when you don't know what it's exactly supposed to look like or how things will turn out.

You can trust Him to tell you what you need to know when you ask. And you can trust Him to give you what you need when you ask, too.

> For everyone who asks receives, and the one who seeks finds, and to the one who knocks it will be opened.
> What father among you, if his son asks for a fish, will instead of a fish give him a serpent;
> or if he asks for an egg, will give him a scorpion?
> If you then, who are evil, know how to give good gifts to your children, how much more will the heavenly Father give the Holy Spirit to those who ask him!"
>
> – Luke 11:10-13

The Lord is still shining on your situation. It might seem like it's taking too long and you've almost given up hoping and praying and watering and expecting, but your answer is on the cusp of blooming. Do not cut it down too early. Don't give up on tending it. He is putting things in order, and answers, solutions, and breakthrough might start unfolding faster than you can believe.

Maybe you thought you would be further by now. You've been in bud for so long, just waiting and waiting, almost to the point you've wondered if you're running out of time. What if there's not enough summer left? What if winter comes too soon? And why does it even matter, if by all rights you should've been in full bloom eons ago, and here you still are, waiting?

Are you just bad at blooming? No. Are you destined to stay folded up and hidden? No. Is it God's will for you to be unhappy, because He loves you very much and has a miserable plan for your life? No.

You are not too late. You're not bad at this. God has joy ahead that would make you laugh at your concerns if you could see it right now.

It feels dark, frustrating, and unrewarding out there some days. You work and work and work and wait, and hope a little, and look...but nope, it's not there yet, so you start all over again, still not seeing the fruit of your labors.

But something's happening underneath. It really is. We'll see it soon. Hang in there.

But thanks be to God, who gives us the victory through our Lord Jesus Christ. Therefore, my beloved brothers, be steadfast, immovable, always abounding in the work of the Lord, knowing that in the Lord your labor is not in vain.

– 1 Corinthians 15:57-58

God will make a way where there seems to be no way.

But be patient! Patience is a poor word, a bitter word for those who have no faith. But you...can you not give God a day, or two days, or whatever time it pleases Him to take, to make justice triumph? Time belongs to Him, and He has promised us so large a portion of it.
– Alessandro Manzoni, *The Betrothed*

Far into the summer, our peonies still hadn't bloomed yet. I anxiously awaited all 41 buds to burst out in bloom (yes, 41, I counted them SO many times) and then I found one of the buds out there, broken, with only two inches of stem.

Sad face. Only forty buds.

I brought it inside and trimmed the stem and searched for the smallest bottle I could find, and discovered an old almond extract bottle in the back of a cabinet. I filled it with water and stuck the peony in. Wondered if it would bloom, or if it was too late, too short, or too dried out to drink water.

Two days later, I refilled the bottle because it was drinking. And the outer petals were just beginning to get the tiniest bit fluffy.

So, hey:

It's not too late.
You're not too small.
You're not beyond hope.

You just need to be thirsty, and drink.

We need to abide in the Living Water, in the word, praying without ceasing.

Like that snapped-off bud, you might even bloom before all the others who were never broken, because proximity to the caregiver speeds up our progress.

We bloom after brokenness. And it's not too late for you, either.

Who is like the Lord our God, who is seated on high,
who looks far down on the heavens and the earth?

He raises the poor from the dust
and lifts the needy from the ash heap, to make them sit
with princes, with the princes of his people.

He gives the barren woman a home, making her the joyous
mother of children. Praise the Lord!

– Psalm 113:5-9

A word about that...I did not always think I would be a
mom. Even when we started having kids, we had to fight
for it; our first baby had a traumatic birth and we lost our
second baby. That's when we first started looking into
adoption, and I realized that was hard, too.

Some things just aren't easy. Parenting and motherhood
are some of those things.

But God turns the impossible on its head. The unlikely
woman becomes a mother. The barren become fruitful. The
lonely are put in families. The broken are made whole.
Confusion becomes clear. The trampled learn boundaries.
The poor become rich. The slave becomes free...and then
they help free others.

What is your impossible, that God wants to use to bring
freedom to many? Because His redemption in us is never
just for us. It is the tiny speck of yeast that grows through
the whole Kingdom.

You can trust Him. Yes, He's teaching you perseverance. But He's not teaching you to be miserable, resigned, or crestfallen. He's teaching you how faithful, loving, good, and creative He is.

> Remember not the former things,
> nor consider the things of old.
> Behold, I am doing a new thing; now it springs forth,
> do you not perceive it? I will make a way in the wilderness
> and rivers in the desert.
>
> – Isaiah 43:18-19

So you have been waiting and waiting and waiting. And now this: Just a little movement, so small it's almost insulting. One petal unfolds, sticking out awkwardly, while everything else is still tightly closed.

Is this a joke?

Doesn't God know you need so much more? You have been running and running, and this small bump of a reward doesn't even come close to what you were hoping for.

Or maybe after a long, dormant season of waiting and enduring, pushing through and trusting, you've finally seen the first small spurts of growth. Nothing impressive, but you tell yourself it's okay to start small. Starting small is normal and healthy, you remember.

But then those spurts die off, and again there's nothing for a while. It looks like dormancy again. Hoping is hard and disappointment and discouragement are getting louder and harder to fight off. But you persevere.

And then, another tiny movement. No bigger than the first ones.

Here's the fulcrum that decides which way the situation tilts:

Will you be grateful and offer the sacrifice of praise? Or will you complain and entertain the doubts and discouragement of the enemy's hissing?

We lose nothing by continuing to trust, moving forward in steadfast diligence. There is much happening underground where the roots are growing.

And let us not grow weary of doing good, for in due season we will reap, if we do not give up.

– Galatians 6:9

That baby step forward seems so insignificant, the encouragement so small. A door barely opened. Will it be enough? Will it even make an impact? Will it be worth the effort, will anyone notice? Will it even matter?

Give it time. Wait and hope.

> And now, O Lord, for what do I wait?
> My hope is in you.
>
> – Psalm 39:7

He sees you when small steps forward cause you to grieve, because it seems like they ought to be bigger steps forward by now...or they ought not to have been needed at all because the circumstances should never have happened. You're not in trouble for having mixed feelings over progress that restores the regress of hard situations. It's okay to be both grateful for the progress and grieved over its necessity.

He is doing something in both the grief and the gratitude.

> But Mary stood weeping outside the tomb,
> and as she wept she stooped to look into the tomb.
> And she saw two angels in white, sitting where the body
> of Jesus had lain, one at the head and one at the feet.
> They said to her, "Woman, why are you weeping?"
> She said to them, "They have taken away my Lord,
> and I do not know where they have laid him."
>
> – John 20:11-13

So can you praise Him in this small thing?

Can you shun disappointment for a minute and refuse to listen to the lies of discouragement long enough to thank Him for this movement?

You want to, because future movement depends on it. Our worship will make the difference between this thing firing up or fizzling out.

> Blessed are those whose strength is in you,
> in whose heart are the highways to Zion.
> As they go through the Valley of Baca
> they make it a place of springs;
> the early rain also covers it with pools.
> **They go from strength to strength;**
> each one appears before God in Zion.
>
> – Psalm 84:5-7

And hey, friend...of course it doesn't look like it should yet. Things are just getting started.

Therefore, beloved,
since you are waiting for these,
be diligent to be found by him
without spot or blemish, and at peace.
And count the patience of our Lord
as salvation...

– 2 Peter 3:14–15a

The peonies finally fully bloomed and we put them all over the house. It took us three years before we made the astonishing and delightful discovery that our cats, who will eat every other plant in the house except for the thorny aloes and citrus trees, also have no interest in eating peonies.

So now the peonies go everywhere. Dozens of them. Hallelujah.

And the thing about peonies is that they force you to bring them in to enjoy them. They're so heavy that unless staked to high heaven, they fall to the ground and lay on the grass, especially during rain. So rather than leave them to rot, you clip them and bring them in to enjoy as long as you can...and you display them in all the high places available, until three years later you finally realize it's safe to put them wherever you want. So you do.

And you feel spoiled at the bounty and the freedom to put them all over the place after restricting yourself for so long...and then you wonder if there's anything else you've unnecessarily restricted in your life, or if there's anything else you've staked to high heaven that you could be

enjoying more. Some of those things you've propped up at a safe distance could be experienced more fully if they fell over in front of you and begged you to do so.

Because those peonies aren't the only things that last for just a brief season.

And now, little children, abide in Him,
so that when He appears we may have confidence
and not shrink back in shame at His coming.

– 1 John 2:28

it's not about your feelings (or anyone else's, either)

Tomorrow has not defeated you already. Today and yesterday didn't defeat you, either.

Your regrets have not defeated you. Here's why:

> Who shall separate us from the love of Christ?
> Shall tribulation, or distress, or persecution, or famine,
> or nakedness, or danger, or sword? As it is written,
> "For your sake we are being killed all the day long;
> we are regarded as sheep to be slaughtered."
> No, in all these things we are more than conquerors
> through him who loved us.
>
> – Romans 8:35-37

...and...

> There is therefore now no condemnation for those who are in Christ Jesus.
>
> – Romans 8:1

But does it seem like you've worked and worked for nothing, and you're afraid people see your incompletion? Maybe you've felt alone, or that you've failed. Sometimes we feel seen in all the wrong ways because what's incomplete is obvious and on display, and what's been going on under the surface is not.

Maybe you've been afraid that you stand out in the worst ways and don't fit in anywhere.

But here's the truth, because our feelings can be liars, and they're easily manipulated by the enemy:

You're not incomplete, and you're not a failure. You're just not done yet. Get back to work and finish.

Yes, it feels like too much, like it's too hard and there's too far to go. But God has created a wrinkle in the path to shorten the distance for you. Start walking and watch what happens. You haven't gone too far in the wrong direction to turn back.

Also, God sees you and has prepared a tribe for you. You are not standing out in the worst ways; you are a missing piece they've needed, and you'll fit perfectly in the space that's waiting for you. Reach for the thing you know is there, even if you can't see it yet.

It is not a matter of feelings. Our feelings are devious; high tide and low tide. They try to be the boss but they often have no idea what the big picture is because they tend to cloud over some really important facts.

Romans 8 is a really good place to camp out right now to get those facts. So is Psalm 46. So are a lot of places.

Run to the Word and know the Lord is moving. We can trust Him.

But God, being rich in mercy,
because of the great love with which he loved us,
even when we were dead in our trespasses,
made us alive together with Christ
—by grace you have been saved—
and raised us up with him and seated us with him
in the heavenly places in Christ Jesus,
so that in the coming ages he might show
the immeasurable riches of his grace in kindness
toward us in Christ Jesus.

For by grace you have been saved through faith.
And this is not your own doing; it is the gift of God,
not a result of works, so that no one may boast.

For we are his workmanship,
created in Christ Jesus for good works,
which God prepared beforehand,
that we should walk in them.

– Ephesians 2:4-10

And another thing (this is me coming back to finish the argument after slamming the door) – just because things look bleak and hopeless doesn't mean they are. How many times in stories or history or the Bible have you seen everything look like all is lost, only to turn out better than you would've imagined?

The Cross and the Resurrection.
Haman's attack, and Esther's favor.
The Battle of Little Round Top.
The Battle of Trenton.
Gandalf and the Balrog.
Aslan and the White Witch.
Omaha Beach.

The Lord is not done in your situation, either.

Some things will be worse than you expect, true. But that's no reason to dread them or lose hope, because some things will also be better.

Dread and pessimism are flimsy weapons. Hope-grounded faith is undefeated.

The Lord is not done with you. Just because it looks like it's over doesn't mean it's over. He has amazing plans for you in the days, weeks, and years to come. Things you would never imagine. Things that if He told you, you would not believe Him.

So He's not telling you yet. But someday soon, you'll start to believe again. He'll show you things that will make it undeniable.

No, in all these things we are more than conquerors
through him who loved us.
– Romans 8:37

It might be that He's waiting for everyone else to finish
their time in the sun, so you will stand out all the brighter.

You don't need to worry about winter, or other imagined
deadlines; you have more time than you think. He holds all
the time, and He loves you more than you know.

That breakthrough you've been working for has seemed so
far away and impossible, as if by the time you get there it
might be too late. But it's not, and it won't be. You are not
running out of time when you are waiting for God's perfect
timing.

In His mercy, He often gives us no choice but to wait. He
knows what's good for us, and He knows we might sacrifice
the good for the easy when we start to feel desperate.

Yours is the day, yours also the night;
you have established the heavenly lights and the sun.
You have fixed all the boundaries of the earth;
you have made summer and winter.
– Psalm 74:16-17

So He gives us a million choices except this one: He doesn't let us choose the timing. He can work with all kinds of our fumbling and learning and risking and trying again, and **He's not afraid of our failures because when they are rooted in obedience they are actually successes,** even though it may not look that way to us in the moment.

He can work with all of our imperfect efforts, but He alone holds the timing for completion. He's not teasing us with riddles in order to achieve breakthrough. He's preparing us to steward the upgrade.

Therefore do not be anxious, saying, 'What shall we eat?'
or 'What shall we drink?' or 'What shall we wear?'
For the Gentiles seek after all these things,
and your heavenly Father knows that you need them all.
But seek first the kingdom of God and his righteousness,
and all these things will be added to you.

– Matthew 6:31-33

Jesus, You're good. And we trust You. But what is that hymn? "Oh, for grace to trust You more." We need that grace. That breakthrough that comes and rewards us after long, hard waiting and believing and trusting when we cannot see. We need the grace of victory that only You can achieve; we've done everything we know to do and all we have left is to stand.

So we're standing. Give us the grace to trust You more, so we can shout in triumph, "See, world? I told You He said so and He never fails to come through."

Here's a bold, no-fail move:

If you are waiting for God to do something you've been waiting a long time for, try asking Him for the thing you've been afraid to ask Him for. And if you can't think of what that is, pray this: *Lord, I invite You to tell me what I've been afraid to ask of You.*

Just do it. Don't hem and haw or overthink it. Give Him permission. Because He moves, but He does not push. So tell Him He is welcome, and unlock the door.

Hope deferred makes the heart sick,
but a desire fulfilled is a tree of life.
Whoever despises the word brings destruction on himself,
but he who reveres the commandment will be rewarded.
The teaching of the wise is a fountain of life,
that one may turn away from the snares of death.

– Proverbs 13:12-14

Where you've been feeling stretched, the Lord is about to simplify things as you trust Him in this you've held back in.

Some of the answers are going to come from directions and changes you've resisted, but as you yield, peace will settle and confirmation will be obvious. You'll feel relief in the same place you've been digging in your heels for years, because He's showing you He can work through (and with) changes you've been resisting.

The Lord is bringing a holy "I told you so" and you'll love it as soon as you surrender to it.

> For my thoughts are not your thoughts,
> neither are your ways my ways, declares the Lord.
> For as the heavens are higher than the earth, so are my
> ways higher than your ways and my thoughts than your
> thoughts.

> For as the rain and the snow come down from heaven
> and do not return there but water the earth, making it
> bring forth and sprout, giving seed to the sower and bread
> to the eater, so shall my word be that goes out from my
> mouth;
> it shall not return to me empty, but it shall accomplish
> that which I purpose, and shall succeed in the thing
> for which I sent it.

> **For you shall go out in joy and be led forth in peace;**
> the mountains and the hills before you shall break forth
> into singing, and all the trees of the field shall clap their
> hands.

> – Isaiah 55:8-12

an Alaskan weather report for the one facing a storm

Tiny new green leaves and stormy skies. Growth that thrives on rain. Buds overcoming their shyness, and boldly doubling their size every day.

Those buds didn't shrink back during the short hailstorm. They plowed ahead, doing what they were made to do.

Do you feel the stretching and growth of a new season? Dark clouds are coming closer and it seems like bad timing – are you strong enough to withstand? Will you know what to do?

Is it a sign that this *isn't* breakthrough? Or maybe an indication you're not supposed to grow in this direction? Or...maybe the clouds are there because it's time to grow. You abide, so you know what to do. You need to keep doing it and not shrink back. You are meant to thrive in the rain, too.

Jesus, help us to grow through obstacles today. Focus us in spite of distraction, help us move boldly in the face of fear. We're clothed with Your Spirit so we reject fear, trusting You and walking in the authority You give us to pray with power and change the world around us.

Fear not, little flock,
for it is your Father's good pleasure to give you the kingdom.

– Luke 12:32

For I consider that the sufferings of this present time
are not worth comparing with the glory
that is to be revealed to us.

For the creation waits with eager longing
for the revealing of the sons of God.

For the creation was subjected to futility, not willingly,
but because of him who subjected it, in hope that
the creation itself will be set free from its bondage to
corruption and obtain the freedom of the glory of the
children of God.

For we know that the whole creation has been groaning
together in the pains of childbirth until now.

And not only the creation, but we ourselves, who have the
firstfruits of the Spirit, groan inwardly as we wait eagerly
for adoption as sons, the redemption of our bodies.

For in this hope we were saved.

Now hope that is seen is not hope.
For who hopes for what he sees?
But if we hope for what we do not see,
we wait for it with patience.

– Romans 8:18-25

That obstacle ahead? You are meant to conquer it. God allowed something in front of you to overcome so you can be an overcomer. We become overcomers by having something to conquer.

Have you memorized this one yet? It's a good one:

Who shall separate us from the love of Christ?
Shall tribulation, or distress, or persecution, or famine,
or nakedness, or danger, or sword?

As it is written,
"For your sake we are being killed all the day long;
we are regarded as sheep to be slaughtered."
**No, in all these things we are more than conquerors
through him who loved us.**

– Romans 8:35-37

You can tackle tomorrow. You will endure. You will overcome.

You are infused with the Word, and the Spirit of the living God dwells in you. He will give you the words and composure and wisdom you need. And you'll know He moved through you and saved the day because you put your trust in Him. Obey and watch.

Humble yourselves, therefore, under the mighty hand of God so that at the proper time he may exalt you, casting all your anxieties on him, because he cares for you.

Be sober-minded; be watchful. Your adversary the devil prowls around like a roaring lion, seeking someone to devour. Resist him, firm in your faith, knowing that the same kinds of suffering are being experienced by your brotherhood throughout the world.

– 1 Peter 5:6-9

You have seen what you are in Christ, now take your place as a prayer warrior. Make hell fear you. Make heaven glad. Fill hearts of men with joy witnessing your winning prayer life. Healing the sick is His will. Saving the lost is His will. Breaking satan's dominion over men is His will.

Praying for ministers and missionaries is His will...Now swing free in your prayer life. Be big! Honor the Word. Dare to do exploits for Him.

– E.W. Kenyon, *In His Presence*

quick reality check

Not everything that happens in the world is the Lord's will.

But we hear the opposite fairly often, from the pulpit and books and popular podcasts. I once heard a speaker say he believed that everything in the world that ever happens is all part of God's plan and purpose for our lives.

But that's not true; it's completely unbiblical. It's also a slippery way of accusing the Lord of perpetuating evil.

Yes, sometimes He allows things...but consider how much He prevents that we are completely unaware of.

Yes, He takes what the enemy means for evil and He turns it for good (see Romans 8:28)...but no, that doesn't mean that everything that happens in the world is His will.

God gives humans free will. Sometimes humans do evil things that the Lord never sanctions.

To say that everything that happens is part of God's will and plan is to tell a rape victim that the Lord is okay with what happened to her. It is to tell an abused child that they need to suck it up and deal because this is part of the Lord's plan. It is to tell the grieving parent who lost their child to cancer or a drunk driver that this, too, is the Lord's will.

Someone who says those things has not spent much time with God or in His word. Those beliefs (which are actually pious-sounding accusations) are completely against His character, and lies from the enemy.

Here's what the Word says He is:

The Lord is gracious and merciful,
slow to anger and abounding in steadfast love.
The Lord is good to all,
and his mercy is over all that he has made.
– Psalm 145:8-9

The Lord is not slow to fulfill his promise as some count slowness, but is patient toward you, not wishing that any should perish, but that all should reach repentance.
– 2 Peter 3:9

Do not be deceived, my beloved brothers.
Every good gift and every perfect gift is from above,
coming down from the Father of lights, with whom
there is no variation or shadow due to change.
– James 1:16-17

This is the message we have heard from him
and proclaim to you, that **God is light,
and in him is no darkness at all.**
– 1 John 1:5

So if God doesn't want evil to happen, why doesn't He prevent it?

He often does and we are completely oblivious. And also, **He also put us here to help prevent things, too:** We are to partner with Him in this work. We are to act and intercede to prevent evil - not to condone it or shrug our shoulders and say it is His will.

He is a good father, not an abuser. He loves you. He has a good, beautiful, holy, joy-filled plan for your life, for this season, and for the situation you're facing.

Sometimes we come up with good reasons for why we're going through a particular trial. Since we know God has a reason for everything, and everything works for good, we convince ourselves that this situation must be part of God's plan, since He loves us very much and wants us to suffer miserably for His sake.

Really. Many of us grew up believing a bunch of half-truths, and they center around that one.

When we come up with reasons for why we're going through something, we sometimes end up agreeing with the circumstance, which often was never God's will at all. Sickness is not His will. Abuse is not His will. Trauma is not His will. Just because He can make good come from anything – and He does, remember Romans 8:28? – it doesn't mean that He wanted the bad thing to happen in the first place.

You keep mentioning that chapter, Romans 8. What is it, anyway? Okay, here you go:

**And we know that for those who love God
all things work together for good,
for those who are called according to his purpose.**

For those whom he foreknew he also predestined
to be conformed to the image of his Son,
in order that he might be the firstborn among many
brothers.

And those whom he predestined he also called,
and those whom he called he also justified,
and those whom he justified he also glorified.

**What then shall we say to these things?
If God is for us, who can be against us?**

– Romans 8:28-32

We don't have to make excuses for our situations, or give good reasons for them, or try to explain them away. We might be in a really crappy season that has no excuse other than that we fight a real enemy in a fallen world, and this place is a cleanup operation.

But we also serve the one real God who loves and cares for us, and equips us, and covers us with His righteousness and favor, and calls us His own. He has good plans for us, and that's what we need to agree with.

slow progress is preparation, not punishment

your God sends you to us. ⁶Whether it is good or bad, we will obey the voice of the LORD our God to whom we are sending you, that it may be well with us when we obey the voice of the LORD our God." *Jeremiah had to wait,*
⁷ <u>At the end of ten days</u> the word of the LORD came to Jeremiah. ⁸Then he summoned *too.* Johanan the son of Kareah and all the commanders of the forces who were with him, and all the people from the least to the greatest,

If you're still waiting for an answer from the Lord, you're in good company. (This is from Jeremiah chapter 42.)

The Lord is not unaware of your need and He's not ignoring you.

He knows you don't see the way through. But He *does* see the way through. He is making a way where there seems to be no way. Keep your eyes on Him, not the impossibilities. Do not worship the problem by magnifying it; magnify the One who makes a way.

You're not behind.
Breakthrough is not overdue.

You cannot miss the promise
because He orchestrates it.
You can rest in His timing and
trust Him.

Do not look at the waves. Don't
give the enemy the satisfaction
of your prolonged attention.
Your eyes are on Jesus.

Keep looking at Him as you tell
the waves to be still – He gave
you the authority to do what
He did, remember? – and take
the step forward He's called
you to.

Therefore the Lord waits
to be gracious to you,
and therefore he exalts himself
to show mercy to you.

For the Lord is a God of
justice;
blessed are all those who wait
for him.

– Isaiah 30:18

You know those things that don't make sense? The ones that aren't adding up right: A plus B ought to equal C but instead it's equaling negative five or something? Even though all the right components are there, it still isn't turning out.

Why have things been so slow, so small, when you know they should've been so big?

Did the Lord forget? Is He angry with you? Did He decide you don't really deserve it?

No. He's growing your wings.

He's teaching you to see, and to be alert, and to recognize that some things around you are not just what they seem.

He's making you strong, and preparing you for exploits.

Things will speed up soon enough, and when they do, you'll be ready because you surrendered to this process of growth and preparation.

> For God alone, O my soul, wait in silence,
> for my hope is from him.
> He only is my rock and my salvation, my fortress;
> I shall not be shaken.
> On God rests my salvation and my glory;
> my mighty rock, my refuge is God.
>
> – Psalm 52:5-7

For who is God, but the Lord?
And who is a rock, except our God?–
the God who equipped me with strength
and made my way blameless.
He made my feet like the feet of a deer
and set me secure on the heights.
He trains my hands for war,
so that my arms can bend a bow of bronze.

You have given me the shield of your salvation,
and your right hand supported me,
and your gentleness made me great.
You gave a wide place for my steps under me,
and my feet did not slip.

– Psalm 18:31-36

It doesn't make sense because you are only seeing part of what's going on. And part of what you're seeing is misleading and meant to discourage you. Don't fall for it.

Just like stepping on the scale when someone else is putting weight on it, the numbers you are seeing aren't the full picture and many of them are false.

Don't put all your trust in the numbers or other things you can see. Put your trust in God who hears you and knows you and answers prayer. He is answering it. Don't let discouragement cause you to give up when victory is so close.

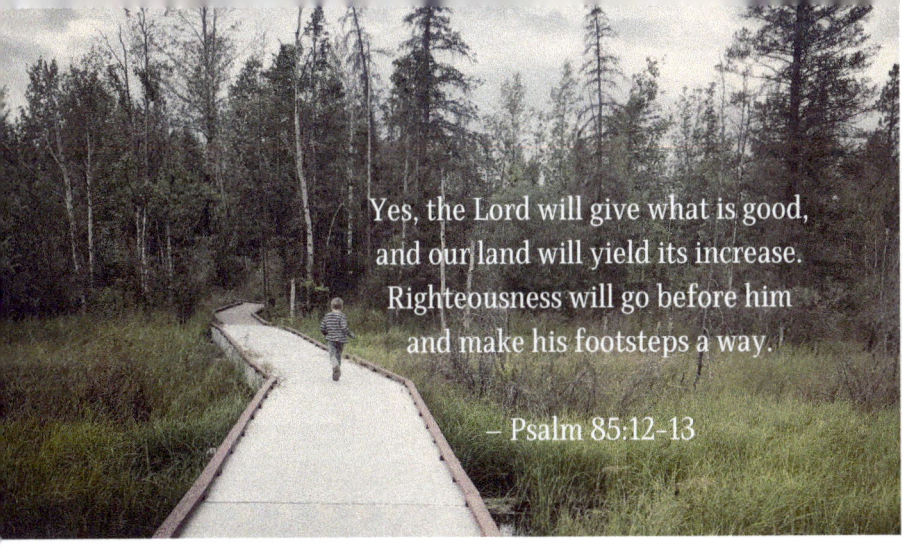

Yes, the Lord will give what is good,
and our land will yield its increase.
Righteousness will go before him
and make his footsteps a way.

– Psalm 85:12-13

Good and upright is the Lord;
therefore he instructs sinners in the way.
He leads the humble in what is right,
and teaches the humble his way.
All the paths of the Lord are steadfast love and faithfulness,
for those who keep his covenant and his testimonies.

– Psalm 25:8-10

The Lord sees those things you've been quiet about and trying to be brave for. He knows you've been inwardly wilting, trying to stand tall but feeling like liquid inside, unsure of how much longer you can go before collapsing.

He has no intention of letting you collapse, though. And He's not playing games, testing to see how far you can go. He knows. He's not some scientist experimenting on you like a lab rat.

He knows how far you can go. So He's preparing you to be there.

Think about that for a second. You can trust Him with change, and with your future, and with your family as you get there, and beyond.

You can trust Him to be good to you during the whole process.

> Grace, mercy, and peace will be with us,
> from God the Father and from Jesus Christ
> the Father's Son, in truth and love.
>
> – 2 John 1:3

The Lord accepts us fully, knowing that we will need time and experience to work out our imperfections. Our failures do not surprise Him. If they surprise us, it is only because we have too high an opinion of ourselves.

– Dr. Henry Cloud, *Changes That Heal*

The Lord is near. He hasn't turned away. He's not a narcissistic parent who is never satisfied.

He is preparing you. Strengthening you. Equipping you. **This season of difficulty and stretching is an honor, not a punishment.**

Strengthen the weak hands, and make firm the feeble knees.
Say to those who have an anxious heart, "Be strong; fear not!
Behold, your God will come with vengeance, with the
recompense of God. He will come and save you."

– Isaiah 35:3-4

It feels like loss when things change, but it's gain, too.
"Character is what we get when we don't get what we want"
is true...except that really, deep down, we *do* want the
character. We just don't want to journey through pain or
disappointment or loss to get it.

This is a journey that Jesus walked though, too.

And do you see how He is letting you in to see the inner
place, where most people aren't willing to go? He's showing
you the place in His heart where He also went through
change that felt like loss. Betrayals, misunderstandings,
moves, and new directions. Rejection, people changing,
culture shifting. He was above it all but He was also in it,
just like us.

And He's not wasting any of this. You surrender it and keep
abiding, pressing forward through pain and uncertainty. He
is causing all of it for your good, whatever the enemy
intended.

And we know that all things work together for good
to those who love God, to those who are the called
according to His purpose.

– Romans 8:28

But also for this very reason, giving all diligence, add to your faith virtue, to virtue knowledge, to knowledge self-control, to self-control perseverance, to perseverance godliness, to godliness brotherly kindness, and to brotherly kindness love. For if these things are yours and abound, you will be neither barren nor unfruitful in the knowledge of our Lord Jesus Christ.

— 2 Peter 5-8

pressing toward the full promise

We had bacon-wrapped jalapeños for dinner and I ate the leftovers for breakfast. In lieu of a photo, just imagine how amazing they are: jalapeños filled with a cream cheese mixture, wrapped in bacon. Go ahead and swoon. Sometimes, though, the bacon doesn't stay wrapped, and you get a naked jalapeño. But that's okay; stuffed with cream cheese, it's still good.

So I ate that one first and then realized the bacon that went with it was buried under the other jalapeños. And here's the super spiritual point I'm getting at: A lot of us have been cruising along, pressing forward in gratitude while knowing we were still missing something that ought to be there.

And gratitude is good.

But so is finding the whole package that Jesus paid for.

So here's a reminder if you've been pressing toward breakthrough and seeing glimpses of it, but not full victory: There is bacon ahead.

The Lord never fails to deliver on His promises. Sometimes we miss them, deny them, or refuse to take them. Sometimes the timing is not our favorite. Sometimes there's attack and delay. But the promises are all Yes and Amen in Jesus.

For all the promises of God find their Yes in him. That is why it is through him that we utter our Amen to God for his glory. And it is God who establishes us with you in Christ, and has anointed us, and who has also put his seal on us and given us his Spirit in our hearts as a guarantee.

– 2 Corinthians 1:20-22

This is the view out our kitchen window. See the snow? It's not bad. In early winter it's beautiful and exciting, but by April and May it's sort of a drag. Not terrible though, we can live with it.

We can endure. If we had to, we could live with it as long as necessary.

Hang onto that thought, because here's a word for some of you:

You are enduring something right now that is lasting longer than it ought to. It is less than God's perfect design for you.

A lot of people are going through that actually, but here's where it gets specific:

You know what it takes to make the snow melt, but you've resigned yourself to perpetual winter because it doesn't seem as bad as the cost of obedience.

Is that you? Be brave and keep reading. Resist the urge to close this. There's sunshine ahead, and no condemnation. Just conviction, but it comes with freedom, and relief, and the glory of summer.

You've decided to settle and endure because it seems more comfortable or safe than what the Lord asked you to do, as the vessel He flows through. And what is very dangerous about that is your heart is becoming cold and numb to hearing Him as you've continued to lean on reasons that justify disobedience.

Friend...you are denying spring. There is so much progress in front of you, and beauty, and warmth, and joy. You don't want to miss out on them. **They are worth the cost.** His smile over you is worth the cost. His hand of protection over you is worth the cost.

We think we can just endure, but in His mercy He will drive us back to Him because the winter will become unbearable. It's a natural consequence; our disobedience moves us out from under the hand of His protection. He didn't remove it – we did. And we may think we can handle snow and cold temperatures for several more months, but that's not what we'll get.

We're not signing up for the status quo. We're signing up for 40 below zero and hurricane force winds.

Not at first, of course, but if we persist in stubbornness, they are coming.

So friend, if you know what you've disobeyed in, confess it right now. It only takes seconds: *Jesus, I'm sorry for ____.* And then take your first step of obedience back in that direction, right now, even if it's only praying, *Lord, help me remember to _____ in the morning.*

And if you don't know what it is but you have a vague suspicion you've grown numb in some area, ask Him right now: *Lord, reveal again what You want me to hear and do. I'm sorry for disobeying and I want to hear You again.*

Then listen. Be willing to hear the thing you don't want to hear – even the thing you realize you're dreading – and surrender it. It may not be the thing He's leading you to do, but even if it is, it's far better than perpetual winter.

But don't go digging around your soul with a garden trowel, determined to find something. Let Him do the work; it's your job to listen if He reveals something, and then obey.

That thing that's triggering fear isn't really the threat you think it is. It's pushing your buttons and making you feel vulnerable in unexpected ways, but you are safe, loved, and secure.

Look at the root of why it's alarming you. That will show you the real issue at hand that you probably need to process and pray about. The thing you've been fearing is just a puffed up version of that, blown out of proportion, as the enemy has tried to play havoc on your thoughts and weak spots. Don't give into him. What's the truth?

You have the mind of Christ. You have been blessed with every spiritual blessing. You are seated with Christ. You are more than a conqueror.

You hear that? You are the one striking fear into the enemy. Do not let him bluff you into believing it's the other way around.

Now to Him who is able to keep you from stumbling, and to present you faultless before the presence of His glory with exceeding joy, to God our Savior...

...Who alone is wise, be glory and majesty, dominion and power, both now and forever. Amen.

– Jude 24-25

That thing you've been dreading might actually end up being a huge step forward for you. It might actually be a huge relief.

So watch your attitude and refuse to waste time in dread. Pray about your concern but move forward in what God is telling you to do so you can partner with Him. Choosing to dread does the opposite; it means partnering with fear and giving it permission. Choose obedience and trust, and give God permission to move in your life instead. We have to surrender to Him to win.

> Teach me your way, O Lord,
> and lead me on a level path because of my enemies.
>
> Give me not up to the will of my adversaries;
> for false witnesses have risen against me,
> and they breathe out violence.
>
> I believe that I shall look upon the goodness of the Lord
> in the land of the living!
>
> Wait for the Lord; be strong,
> and let your heart take courage; wait for the Lord!
>
> – Psalm 27:11-14

Friend, if you are dreading the day tomorrow, or some day up ahead...He is right there, with you, ahead of you, and behind you.

If the tasks on your list seem like too much, or the kids are too much, or the people are too much, or the pain and conflict are too much, just go slow.

Watch and listen for what the Lord is up to. He wants to show you something in the overwhelm as you persevere. There's joy and peace and certainty there as we abide.

And when we find it, we'll also find ourselves dreading our tomorrows less. We know we will walk in power as we go through them.

The Lord is already holding your days. You do not need to shrink back or fret. He knows and He sees you. He is walking with you, speaking to you, speaking to others on your behalf, and making a way for you.

Every time you trust Him, you protect your path forward. The snow and ice melt; your direction emerges clearly.

"Let not your hearts be troubled. Believe in God; believe also in me. In my Father's house are many rooms. If it were not so, would I have told you that I go to prepare a place for you? And if I go and prepare a place for you, I will come again and will take you to myself, that where I am you may be also. And you know the way to where I am going."

Thomas said to him, "Lord, we do not know where you are going. How can we know the way?"

Jesus said to him, "I am the way, and the truth, and the life. No one comes to the Father except through me. If you had known me, you would have known my Father also. From now on you do know him and have seen him."

— John 14:1-7

Lord, this is Your day, and Your week, and Your agenda. You know all the things on our calendar, and all the things we don't know about that aren't on it yet. We give them all to you. Help us to handle each one well, with joy and peace and wisdom, refusing to dread or stress or strive. Help us hear You and abide as we move through these days, stewarding them well to expand the Kingdom. You have great plans for us, and we will fear no Monday, or Tuesday...or any other day.

Of this gospel I was made a minister
according to the gift of God's grace,
which was given me by the working of his power.

To me, though I am the very least of all the saints,
this grace was given, to preach to the Gentiles
the unsearchable riches of Christ, and to bring to light
for everyone what is the plan of the mystery
hidden for ages in God, who created all things,
so that through the church the manifold wisdom of God
might now be made known to the rulers and authorities
in the heavenly places.

This was according to the eternal purpose that he has
realized in Christ Jesus our Lord, in whom we have boldness
and access with confidence through our faith in him.

– Ephesians 3:7-12

courage for those recovering from trauma

This chapter is not for everyone. And friend, I hope it's not for you, but if it is, hold on and press forward: There's light and freedom at the end of it. If I were with you I would hold your hand as we step forward and tell you it's going to be okay. It is. But even better; He is with you – at your elbow, within your blood, breathing life into your lungs. So here we go.

This is about those situations and circumstances we've written off as hopeless, the ones we've pushed away to the farthest corner possible because they're filled with blackness and despair. Those ones where we're convinced that nothing good is coming of it; the enemy has tried to stop our ears and imaginations to all truth. He's tried to cover our thoughts in that area with bleak resignation.

Part of the problem is that we protect ourselves by willful blindness. We turn off our vision in those areas – we can't avert our eyes exactly, the trauma or pain is too close – but we can numb ourselves to seeing it. *It's too much to deal with right now. I don't know what to do anyway.* The voices are too loud and the disappointments are so crushing. It's too much to face, so we refuse to do so.

We don't even tell ourselves it won't get better; we just accept this as our new less-than reality. We wanted more than this, sure, but well, it wasn't to be. "More than" was not for us. "More than" is for a select few – the rich maybe, or the immensely talented, or the highly favored, or those who were brought up in perfect families with all the right opportunities.

We think maybe it's temporary and that we'll come back to it later when things are easier or safer or clearer, but they never are because we never dealt with them to make them so. And when life started to ease up in the slightest we were so elated by the reprieve that we could not imagine losing it by going back to deal with the dark place.

We wouldn't really have lost the reprieve, of course; that was fear talking. And us listening.

So we live in blackness – not everywhere, of course, but in this one area we've given up on. Other things are mostly okay, and because of the contrast between darkness and light we don't realize the amount of grey that bleeds into our areas of bright color, like so much ash blown by the slightest breath of wind.

The areas near our resignation are soot-smudged and tainted, shadowed by mediocrity we accept by default because of their proximity to the blackness: A hard relationship with a child that bleeds onto all our parenting. A leadership wound that taints our desire to serve. An old trauma that kindles fear into every new relationship.

And we get used to this, and stop thinking about it. We have accepted it like the smells in our house and the hum of the refrigerator.

With enough time, the blackness is so integrated that, should someone question it, we eventually argue on its behalf. We make excuses, defending what the enemy has done in this part of our lives with our own justification, rationalizing away all the insecurities it bubbles up in us. Because, hey, this is our normal. And if our normal isn't okay, we must not be okay.

And we have to be okay, because we know the blackness doesn't get any better – and if we admitted it was supposed to be better, than we'd have to admit we were wrong to accept it in the first place.

Accepting it has been easier. We kicked against that dark shell for a while but it was exhausting, and when we gave up, it covered us like a blanket soaked in chloroform.

It's okay, the enemy hissed. *You just rest here.*

And we did.

You're thinking, I hope, of a situation in your life that has been covered in this kind of darkness. Maybe you're thinking of a multitude of them. What you're thinking of is what the Lord wants to deal with.

You need to know that the enemy will do anything to distract you from acknowledging it, and admitting that the blackness is not okay.

He will fight you every step of the way. And yes, fighting back is exhausting. But if you think about it and just peel back the thinnest layers of his lies to you, you'll realize that the blackness has been sucking the energy and strength you've wanted to give to so many other areas of your life that have been tainted by the shadows of this other issue.

It takes a brave person to hack away at the darkness, to admit the emperor has no clothes, to acknowledge that our acceptance of despair has been an agreement with the one who hates us rather than an agreement with the God who loves us.

It takes one brave thought. One honest admission. One strong moment of clarity to start kicking at the hardened blackness.

We start to think truth. We think, *Hey – it wasn't meant to be this way.*

And a flake of crust loosens from the darkness.

We think, *I'm not going to make excuses anymore about this. This is wrong.*

We start to agree with God. *I'm not destined to live like this. God didn't die for me to be "less than" in my life.*

You realize you are the rich, the immensely talented, the highly favored, the one with the perfect Father who gives you all the right opportunities.

Blessed be the God and Father of our Lord Jesus Christ, who has blessed us in Christ with every spiritual blessing **in the heavenly places**, even as **he chose us in him before the foundation of the world**, that we should be holy and blameless before him. **In love he predestined us for adoption to himself** as sons through Jesus Christ, according to the purpose of his will, to the praise of his glorious grace, with which he has blessed us in the Beloved. **In him we have redemption through his blood, the forgiveness of our trespasses, according to the riches of his grace, which he lavished upon us, in all wisdom and insight making known to us the mystery of his will,** according to his purpose, which he set forth in Christ as a plan for the fullness of time, to unite all things in him, things in heaven and things on earth.

– Ephesians 1:3–10

But then it gets sticky, and all of our paths diverge in their own directions. Relationship issues have their lies to be confronted and healed, lifestyle choices have another set of lies that have to be confronted and healed. Past trauma has its own set of lies that need untangled. And the overlap from one area to another can seem overwhelming and complicated.

This is when we ask Him for the One Thing.

Just one, and He is a gentle, precise teacher. He will give you the most important thing to tackle that you are ready for. He doesn't waste any time on peripherals, but He will also only confront the strongest lie that you are ready to handle.

It's likely the enemy will immediately compound his efforts and lie to you about this because he's terrified you will realize you've been locked in a prison with the key in your possession the entire time. He will tell you it's too much, you can't handle it, it's too painful, you're just not ready. He knows that appealing to our laziness and exhaustion with excuses and rationale works. And he will keep trying it until he realizes it doesn't work on us anymore.

So we must not allow it to work.

We have to ask God, *What is the One Thing?* And He tells us.

Maybe the One Thing is a habit we've held onto that hurt us or our family. We may suddenly realize (or already know) there are a whole host of related habits that are also bringing decay into our lives. But, no matter – He has given us the One Thing, so we acknowledge it. We start there.

Yes, I did/believed/accepted that. Yes, it was wrong. Yes, You made me for more.

Big, deep breath. You did it. Now what?

It depends. Some of us might be tempted to run back to despair and excuses here because the issue at hand really is more about someone else's choices than ours, and we know we can't change them.

If this is the case, there is good news. Ready? You don't have to change them. What you've already acknowledged has moved mountains – not only in your life, but in this other person's life as well. You have moved a barrier out of the way. You've peeled a layer of darkness away and light is emanating beyond – the grey areas nearby are cleaner and brighter already.

As the darkness begins to lift, the Lord allows us to see strength that was won in the hard place.

O you who love the Lord, hate evil!
He preserves the lives of his saints;
he delivers them from the hand of the wicked.
Light is sown for the righteous,
and joy for the upright in heart.

– Psalm 97:10-11

Jesus, I'm praying tonight for the one who is running out of hope and needing to hear Your words. We command the enemy to be silent, the lies to be crushed, the attacks and accusations to dissolve into nothing.

We release peace and wisdom and the ability to hear You again, louder and stronger than before. I pray that we will walk and think and speak in ways that agree with You and Your word, instead of capitulating to the enemy and his lies.

Show us how strong we are, how we are more than overcomers. Help us to not pave the way for the enemy's plans with foolish, hopeless words.

We are shutting off that path and building the road that takes us forward by reading Your word, and agreeing with it.

For God, who said, "Let light shine out of darkness," has shone in our hearts to give the light of the knowledge of the glory of God in the face of Jesus Christ.

– 2 Corinthians 4:6

how (and why) we move out of God's way

We have two citrus trees that our youngest daughter planted when she was a preschooler. We don't know what kind they are; she just collected a bunch of seeds from organic citrus fruits and planted them. Sooo...grapefruit, lemon, lime, orange...no idea. They still don't have flowers or fruit yet, just lots of branches and leaves and thorns.

I don't know if they'll ever bear fruit. I've read several articles; none of them agreed. So we water, and fertilize, and pray.

But one year, after they reached the ceiling and started crowding everything else in the room, I pruned them pretty hard. I wasn't sure they would forgive me, but I knew there was no chance of fruit without it.

And they did forgive me. They both grew again, and they grew fuller, rather than being lanky or spindly.

Friends, have you been planting seed and wondering if there will ever be a harvest? Are you feeling pruned, and you wonder if you'll ever grow again?

And hey, let's be honest and real here: Are you having a hard time forgiving the Gardener or anyone else for the unfruitful season and the pruning?

He knows what He's doing. He doesn't have to research and experiment. He's not afraid of your thorns. And He knows what kind of fruit you'll bear, too.

He's watering and fertilizing and speaking life over you. Pretty soon you're going to hear Him say, "Hey Love...it's time to start bearing fruit."

Our breakthrough is often on the other side of forgiveness. If you're tempted to brush past this, thinking "Oh, that's just not for me, forgiveness is for other people but not me," then this is definitely for you.

Did you know that unforgiveness is a lack of trust in God? It is, because forgiveness trusts that God knows, cares, heals, and brings perfect justice and mercy.

Forgiveness trusts that God is doing something about the pain and the person who caused it, and not demanding our own way in what that dealing looks like.

It's not about feelings. It's about choosing to get out of God's way so He can deal with the one who wounded or offended us. It's also about setting ourselves free.

We don't have to feel forgiving or have all the warm fuzzies. We just have to remind ourselves we've chosen to forgive – over and over and over sometimes, anytime the enemy riles that old pain up again. We also may need to set boundaries, but that's another issue.

You can do this. I can do this. Choose it right now for your freedom, and let go of all bitterness, resentment, and the need to broadcast what happened to you. (This doesn't negate the need to process with someone you can trust, or receive counseling. That's not what I mean here by broadcasting.) But we know we're walking in forgiveness or resentment if we're no longer looking for opportunities to share our offense.

And hey, also: We can forgive ourselves. If God has forgiven us – and He has – we should not presume to have higher standards than He does.

This is a good place to take your impossible prayers, and let your faith light up.

That is why it depends on faith,
in order that the promise may rest on grace
and be guaranteed to all his offspring–
not only to the adherent of the law
but also to the one who shares the faith of Abraham,
who is the father of us all, as it is written,
"I have made you the father of many nations"
–in the presence of the God in whom he believed,
who gives life to the dead
and calls into existence the things that do not exist.

In hope he believed against hope,
that he should become the father of many nations,
as he had been told, "So shall your offspring be."

He did not weaken in faith when he considered his own
body, which was as good as dead
(since he was about a hundred years old),
or when he considered the barrenness of Sarah's womb.

No unbelief made him waver concerning the promise of
God, but **he grew strong in his faith as he gave glory to**
God, fully convinced that God was able to do what he
had promised. That is why his faith was
"counted to him as righteousness."
But the words "it was counted to him"
were not written for his sake alone, but for ours also.
It will be counted to us who believe in him who raised
from the dead Jesus our Lord, who was delivered up
for our trespasses and raised for our justification.

– Romans 4:16-25

Forgiveness is so powerful that God redeemed the world with it when Jesus surrendered to the cross.

So if God is calling you to forgive someone, you have the opportunity to participate in that kind of redemption, too.

As the Holy Spirit walks us through forgiveness, it's okay to step back and pause. You may need to keep some things to yourself, to not unload both barrels, to keep your loose ends and private work to yourself. Yes, be a light on a hill, but also, don't cast your pearls before swine.

It's not restraint and self control if we're being quiet out of fear or laziness. And it's not boldness and justice if we unleashed words when the Lord told us to stop and consider.

He's eager to give us wisdom. He's not leaning over us with His arms crossed, tapping His foot in irritation as we navigate hard situations. He is patient and kind and His love casts out fear. So if you're feeling fear, He's not the source of it.

You can trust Him to finish the work in you, and in others. It's His work, not yours, so forgive quickly and move out of His way so He has room to do it.

Even when we sleep, the Lord can speak to us and reveal things to us. He can also well up in us emotions and affections that align us with Him. In dreams, He can help us have feelings of love toward those we need to forgive, and He can give us tenderness toward people and situations we've been hardened toward.

Of course, not all dreams are from God. The enemy does plenty of infiltrating in our sleep, too.

So tonight, if you have a situation or a person you are struggling with and you cannot summon the feelings and willpower to do what needs to be done – even if what needs to be done is just loving and honoring someone in your heart and thoughts – surrender your rest to God. Ask Him to speak to you and bring you into alignment with Him as you sleep.

You'll wake up encouraged, and you'll know it wasn't you who did it the work. You need Him to move you, so ask Him to do it when you'll put up the least resistance. (And you can ask Him to do this for your kids, too.)

Rejoice in the Lord always;
again I will say, rejoice.
Let your reasonableness be known to everyone.
The Lord is at hand; do not be anxious about anything,
but in everything by prayer
and supplication with thanksgiving
let your requests be made known to God.
And the peace of God, which surpasses all understanding,
will guard your hearts and your minds in Christ Jesus.

– Philippians 4:4-7

You're not bad at forgiving someone just because you still have pain from what they did. If memories keep coming back to you about what happened, it doesn't mean you haven't forgiven.

God isn't asking you to dismiss pain or reality. And when we understand that He forgives those who hurt us (as we are also trying to forgive them), He is not dismissing or forgetting what we went through. He knows. But He's making a way for us to be free and whole – more free and more whole, even – in spite of what happened. He is turning wrong to right, just as rotting compost becomes rich soil.

How someone treats you is less about how they feel about you and more about how they feel about themselves. It's not really about you.

But the same is true for how we treat others – that is about us. How we treat others reflects our own character, not anyone else's.

God defines you. Jesus knew He was who His Father said He was, in spite of accusations and wounds from those around Him. So when we are wounded and others try to define us, we are already defined by your Father, too.

Everything Jesus did reveals who God is. So everything we do should reveal who God is, too. We lead others to Him by our actions, words, and character.

So, you be you: Genuine, humble, learning, and praying.

Abide with the One who sees and knows. Forgive and repent and speak life and keep going. Great days are ahead for the steadfast, faithful, and forgiving.

> ... bearing with one another and,
> if one has a complaint against another,
> forgiving each other; as the Lord has forgiven you,
> so you also must forgive.
>
> – Colossians 3:13

Remember, forgiveness is not a set of nicey-nice feelings we have to drum up or muster. Forgiveness is a choice to move out of God's way so He can bring fullness to correction and justice.

Sometimes the person we have to forgive is ourselves. The sooner we do so, the sooner we realize His correction toward our repentant hearts is not something to fear, but to run toward – as we would to a rescuer, because He is.

Do you want God to move? Then you want to move out of His way and forgive people. This is a good time to do it, and let go of the burden that doesn't belong to you.

So we surrender to forgiveness, trust God with the outcome, and watch things start to finally shift in ways we haven't been able to achieve before.

He who walks righteously and speaks uprightly,
who despises the gain of oppressions,
who shakes his hands, lest they hold a bribe,
who stops his ears from hearing of bloodshed
and shuts his eyes from looking on evil,
he will dwell on the heights;
his place of defense will be the fortresses of rocks;
his bread will be given him; his water will be sure.

– Isaiah 33:15-16

Jesus, protect us as we move about the day today. Help us to give You room to move through us: We will pause when You want to interrupt us, we will notice those You want us to see, and we will speak and do the things You want to speak and do through us.

Help us to remember the little things in the midst of the big things. We know You're near, speaking and leading and loving us.

if you're tired of hearing about beauty for ashes

During worship one night, I saw a picture of a piece of wood that had burned for a while, then was pulled out of the fire, and water was poured over it.

Some of us have burned for a while but the pain became too intense and we withdrew. And in mercy, the Lord poured water on us to soothe the pain and trauma.

And then, cool and charred, we feel we have nothing to show for the burning but ugly scars. No achievement, no victory, just the ugliness of quitting, failure, or disappointment. But there's still the desire to burn. We know we were made for it.

So we fight fear because we've been sitting here in the water and wounding, wondering if the pain is going to be just as bad if we re-enter the fire. Maybe it will be worse.

Maybe we're too wet to burn. Maybe it's too late. Or maybe we have to start all over, from the very beginning, and lose all that time.

But here's the truth: You don't have have to start again at the beginning. You don't have to wait until you're dry and cleaned up again. **The Lord can burn wet wood.**

> [Elijah] said, "Fill four jars with water and pour it on the burnt offering and on the wood." And he said, "Do it a second time." And they did it a second time. And he said, "Do it a third time." And they did it a third time.
>
> And the water ran around the altar
> and filled the trench also with water.
>
> And at the time of the offering of the oblation, Elijah the prophet came near and said, "O Lord, God of Abraham, Isaac, and Israel, let it be known this day that you are God in Israel, and that I am your servant, and that I have done all these things at your word. Answer me, O Lord, answer me, that this people may know that you, O Lord, are God, and that you have turned their hearts back."
>
> Then the fire of the Lord fell and consumed the burnt offering and the wood and the stones and the dust, and licked up the water that was in the trench.
>
> And when all the people saw it, they fell on their faces and said, "The Lord, he is God; the Lord, he is God."
>
> – 1 Kings 18:33-39

But sometimes it feels like life is ashes and you're so over it that if someone reminded you of the phrase "beauty for ashes" you'd maybe want to punch them.

You know the scripture and the truth and God's promises but you are looking at your situation and seeing total dissonance. The situation you're looking at does not at all reflect those good, amazing, wonderful, fairy tale things.

People ask you how it's going, and everyone knows what "it" is – that thing people are sorry for but really can't help, that thing you've needed breakthrough for and even though it's private, the need is so great that you've opened up and made it public because you desperately need prayer and help. But still, the situation has gone on and on and you're so tired of people asking how you're doing because you just don't want to be known by this one issue anymore.

You're tired of being the person everyone prays for that health situation, that family problem, that financial need, that trauma. It has started to feel less about faith in miracles and more about this being your identity. People look at you with sympathy, but also relief that they're not dealing with what you've been dealing with. Sometimes they'll even say, "Better you than me, I'm not strong enough for that," but you're tired of being strong, too.

Here's some more truth: God likes you as much as them. (Also: Those other people are a mess, too.) And He's entrusting you with more.

He's leading you to a new level of strength that overcomes what you see. He's teaching you to walk in authority not out of immature ease and confidence, but in gritty, hard-won, sober, tested, in-the-trenches faith.

So here, let's look at this with Kingdom eyes:
We are not the situations we're dealing with.

Our circumstances, no matter how long they last, are not our destiny or our lot in life.

We get to choose if we come out of this stronger or weaker, empowered or embittered.

You're not the only one dealing with a really hard thing. But as you pray for others dealing with the same magnitude of hardship, you are paving the way for your own breakthrough.

And when someone else gets breakthrough, your ability to rejoice with them (rather than feeling jealous) changes the trajectory of your situation, because breakthroughs and joy are contagious. It's not a zero sum game; God is not running out of good news.

You will not always be known for this situation. You will be known for overcoming it.

But if Christ is in you, although the body is dead because of sin, the Spirit is life because of righteousness. If the Spirit of him who raised Jesus from the dead dwells in you, he who raised Christ Jesus from the dead will also give life to your mortal bodies through his Spirit who dwells in you.

– Romans 8:10-11

don't mistake the middle for the end

It's hard to distinguish colors in the dark.

If you're fighting depression, fear, anxiety, condemnation, or any of their cohorts, remember that not everything you're thinking, feeling, and perceiving reflects reality.

Keep in mind that you're fighting darkness, which obscures colors and lines. It blurs shapes and makes bright things gloomy.

It helps to not take darkness so seriously, to keep in mind that things are lighter and freer and more hopeful than they seem. And knowing that makes a big difference.

> Arise, shine, for your light has come,
> and the glory of the Lord has risen upon you.
> For behold, darkness shall cover the earth, and thick darkness the peoples; but the Lord will arise upon you, and his glory will be seen upon you.
> And nations shall come to your light, and kings to the brightness of your rising.
> – Isaiah 60:1-3

Oh Beloved, did you forget who you are? Equipped and guided, led by a strong hand...looked after, held, watched over, affectionately favored by the King.

And I wonder if you've forgotten that you are a fighter, if the enemy has made you feel like your sword was too dangerous. So instead of wielding it better (which would hurt him) he convinced you to lay it aside entirely to be safe.

But God is not asking us to be safe or protect ourselves; He's the one who is our safety and protection. You are a bold warrior and the Kingdom needs you out there. The enemy is desperate to keep you from the fight.

God is eager to pour out more mercy and grace to you. It's what He paid for, and He wants the full reward of what He died for. So hey, Love...you would be inconsiderate not to take it.

It's the lies of the enemy again that tell you, "Nope, you've had enough, stop getting in line for this, it's someone else's turn." He's hoping we'll fall for that trick again, believing God is too small or too stingy or too limited to do and be everything He really is.

We *have* to ask for more grace and mercy, because He's already made it available to us. To act like we shouldn't take it is to put our judgment above God's.

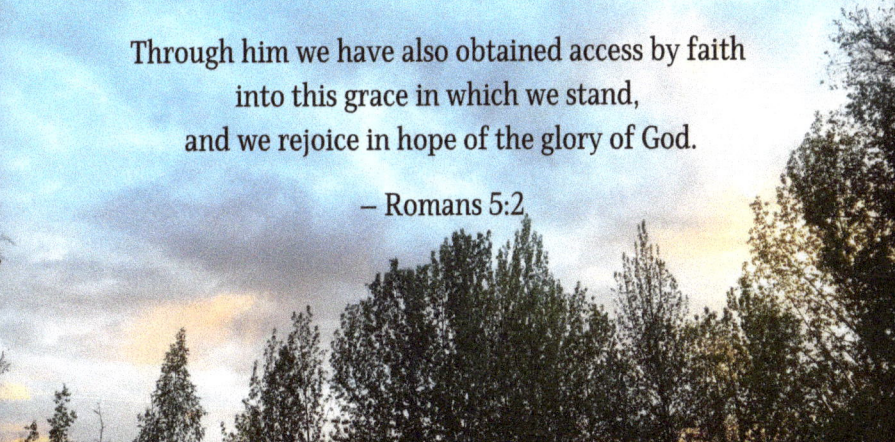

He's a good dad. He knows what we need. He wants us to ask for and receive it.

Through him we have also obtained access by faith
into this grace in which we stand,
and we rejoice in hope of the glory of God.

– Romans 5:2

When anxiety rears up, we tend to feel frantic, like we need to hurry up and do something even though we often have no idea what to do.

But God is not in a rush. That isn't to say He doesn't care, doesn't know our need, or is having fun at our expense. It means He already knows what's on the next page, and He isn't in a hurry to turn to it.

He knows how the answer is going to be revealed, and He knows exactly how stressed out you are in trying to anticipate it while you endure the unknowing.

You know why we're not good at waiting? Because usually answers come so fast we don't have time for anxiety. All the millions of little things that resolve themselves throughout the day (What should we buy for a gift? What should this kid's consequence be? Where will I put the broody chicken?) are not any bigger in His eyes than the big things we're facing right now that also need answers.

We don't think to even trust Him in those small everyday things, but He is just as faithful in the big things. He's showing us that we can trust Him, no matter what.

> The Lord your God is in your midst,
> a mighty one who will save;
> he will rejoice over you with gladness;
> he will quiet you by his love;
> he will exult over you with loud singing.

–Zephaniah 3:17

The Lord knows that you've done what you could, but this situation still hasn't turned out the way you wanted, dreamed, or expected it to. He knows you worked and prayed so hard to have it turn out differently.

It's still turning out, though.

Don't mistake this as the end when it's still the middle. He's not done yet, and neither are you.

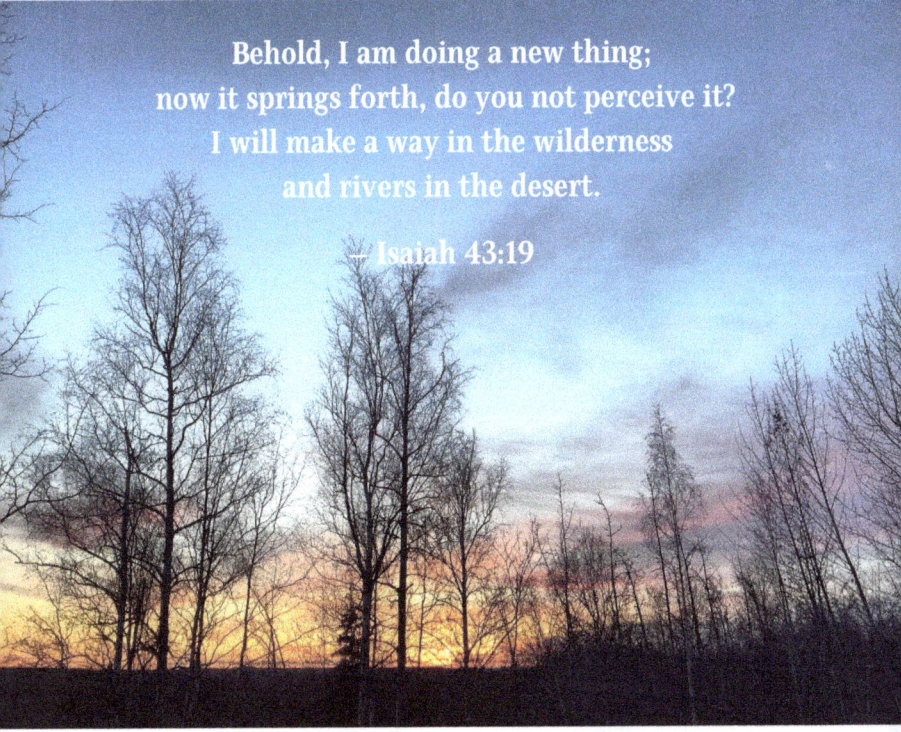

Behold, I am doing a new thing;
now it springs forth, do you not perceive it?
I will make a way in the wilderness
and rivers in the desert.

– Isaiah 43:19

But for you who fear my name, the sun of righteousness shall rise with healing in its wings. You shall go out leaping like calves from the stall.

–Malachi 4:2

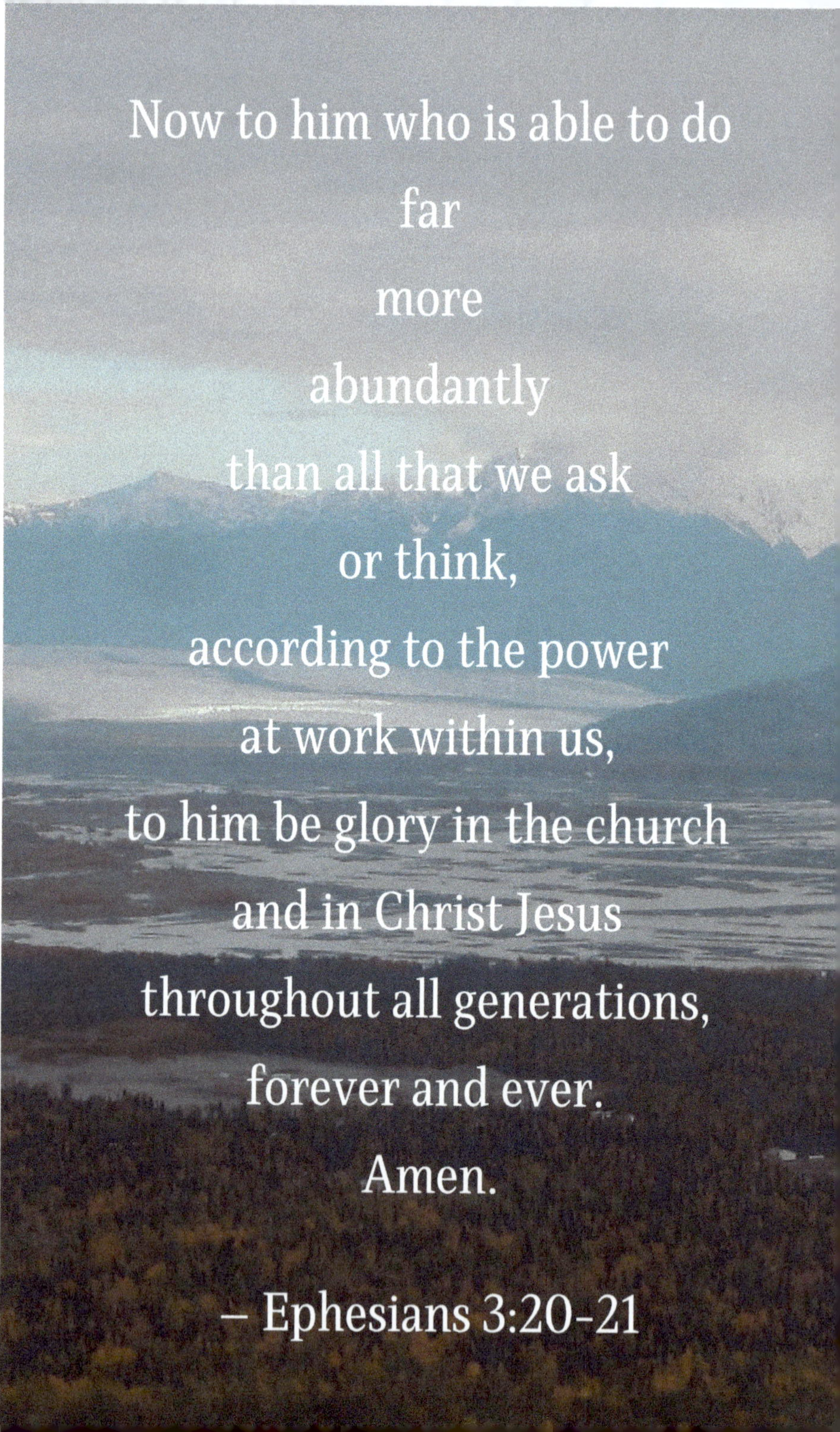

Now to him who is able to do

far

more

abundantly

than all that we ask

or think,

according to the power

at work within us,

to him be glory in the church

and in Christ Jesus

throughout all generations,

forever and ever.

Amen.

– Ephesians 3:20-21

Hi, friend. I'm Shannon Guerra: coffee drinker, mom of eight, wife to Vince, lifelong Alaskan, and accidental selfie taker.

I love sharing God's words with you. But more than that, I want to help equip you to hear Him for yourself, to be in His word, abiding, and knowing Who He is and what His voice sounds like.

Want to know more? Visit copperlightwood.com, where we are pursuing Jesus with raw authenticity and cultivating Kingdom culture, deep and wide, in Southcentral Alaska.

To subscribe to my content, click the green button at https://shannonguerra.substack.com.

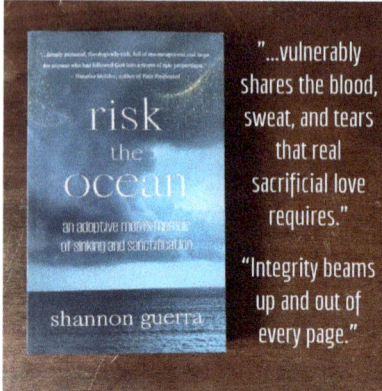

"...vulnerably shares the blood, sweat, and tears that real sacrificial love requires."

"Integrity beams up and out of every page."

"Shannon has written a book every follower of Jesus should read."

"Her fresh approach to praying without ceasing will forever change the way you pray."

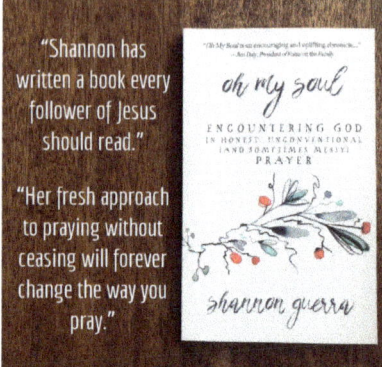

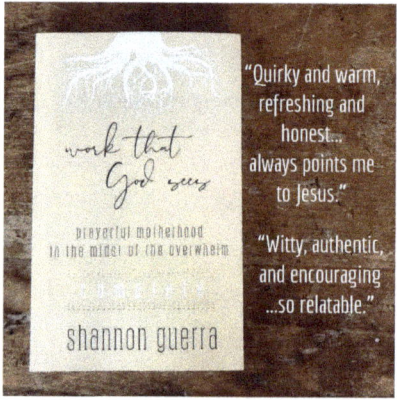

"Quirky and warm, refreshing and honest... always points me to Jesus."

"Witty, authentic, and encouraging ...so relatable."

"...a must-read for anyone who knows an adoptive family."

"It's the practical applications of Biblical text that make me treasure this series."

"Such a healing balm for the weary soul."